In fragments one might be known. Seen from dozens of angles, the mind may move among facets and see the whole. It is, in fact, how *seeing* works in the human brain anyhow. Katherine Indermaur's *I|I* finds rich resonances among these disparate but not discrete shards. Rather a full shape in time and space assembles. Both the "lyric" and the "essay" are fully achieved, home is sought, the self seeks to connect with all of what is beyond.

KAZIM ALI
Judge of the 2022 Deborah Tall Lyric Essay Book Prize

I|I

KATHERINE INDERMAUR

WINNER OF THE 2022 DEBORAH TALL
LYRIC ESSAY BOOK PRIZE

Selected by Kazim Ali

DEBORAH TALL LYRIC ESSAY
BOOK PRIZE SERIES EDITOR

Geoffrey Babbitt

I | I

SENECA REVIEW BOOKS

I

KATHERINE INDERMAUR

Published by Seneca Review Books, an imprint

of Hobart & William Smith Colleges Press

300 Pulteney St., Demarest 101

Geneva, NY 14456

www.hws.edu/senecareview

Seneca Review Books is grateful to Hobart & William
Smith Colleges, Hobart & William Smith Colleges
Press, *Seneca Review*, and the Trias Writer-in-
Residence Program for their generous support.

ISBN: 978-0-910969-07-9

LCCN: 2022942033

Design and composition by Crisis

Author photo by Diane Kelly

Printed in the United States of America

Thank you to the following journals, where excerpts
from *I|I* first appeared, sometimes in different versions:
*COAST|noCOAST, EX/POST Magazine, Gasher, Ghost
Proposal, New Delta Review, Oxidant|Engine, pulpmouth,*
and *Seneca Review.* Thank you to COAST|noCOAST
for publishing part of this book as a chapbook, titled
Facing the Mirror: An Essay, in August 2021.

SRB

N.B. THE TITLE, *I/I*, IS PRONOUNCED
BY REPEATING THE PERSONAL PRONOUN
"I" ONCE AFTER A BRIEF PAUSE.

FOR MOM, THE FIRST WRITER I KNEW

I|I

1

♦

The face signifies the Infinite.

EMMANUEL LEVINAS

I start the fire I suffer.

NARCISSUS, OVID'S
METAMORPHOSES III.465

III

If I could only see more clearly my own seeing—

Mirror. From the Latin *mirare/mirari*, to look at or to be surprised, to look at with wonder. Mirror and miracle are cousins of wonder.

To mirror. To mimic exactly. Two margins and the air between them. And the light to cleave them.

◆

As a child I|I stood staring at the reflection of my|my eyes in the bathroom mirror switching off and on the overhead light. In the on position: the quick closing of the center of my|my black-point eyes, the shock of light swelling the blue. In the off: the center growing dark open to dark open, like ears hoping to listen.

To see our own eyes is to gaze straight at the lag rooted in the loop of light from mind to mirror and back. If I|I blinked quickly enough, I|I could sometimes catch a glimpse of my|my eyes completely shut.

◆

There is no objective mirror.
A looking glass. See? The glass is looking.

Every morning I|I paint my|my self-portrait. I|I paint my|self soft and pink. I|I layer us on.

Mirrors have the tiresome effect of not getting in the way.

◆

Clarity can be distilled from matter is a belief we hold when looking. Not how it is, but how it looks.

How hard it is to continually recognize my|my face.

◆

In German, *Gesicht* means both face and vision, the root *-sicht* an ancestor of sight. Light and sight, sister words. Face as site of first contact. Eye contact. In a mirror, I|I make contact with my|my desire for contact. Eye and I|I,

◆

a between.

3

I|I look in the mirror like it is a type of convincing, staring the facts of my|my existence in a light-echo face like a song sung into a canyon and come back softer, longer.

I|I want light to reveal, but it only travels—passive from the start. Every seeing distorts the world.

◆

The geometry of my|my face is fractal, a Mandelbrot set, the coastline I|I thought I|I'd mapped. The closer I|I look, the more there is to see.

The reward for looking deeply is like an afternoon spent at one window—how the day opens, deepens within a frame. The features of the face are a quiet infinity.

◆

The mirror's between is fracture. Refracted light. What kind of solipsism is this, the self split? Can we even say "I" and remain one? A schism in speaking. I|I as riven as world.

Fracture everything eyetouch.

A practice: At home, early morning, take a pad of sticky notes and a pen. Start in the kitchen. If you can see your face in the object, put a number on the sticky note and stick it to the object. Suggestions: Knives (1-4). Spoons (5-8). Plates (9-19). Bowls (20-28). Rings (29-30). Earrings (30-38). Glitter (39). Mason jar lids (40-44). Perfume bottle tops (45-46). Sunglasses (47-48). Patent leather shoes (49). Belt buckles (50). Hair clips (51). Computer screens (52). The door to the microwave (53). Lids to pots and pans (54-56). Lids to candles (57-59). The teakettle (60). The mirror (61).

The final sticky note is the number of faces looking back. How many you you live with. How many you you are.

One of the cardinal virtues, Prudence, is often signified by a beautiful young woman holding a mirror. Originally conceived by Plato to be a useful virtue for those with the power to make decisions, Prudence is the mirror on the wall telling you the fairest girl is someone else.

The mirror enables self-correction, like smoothing my hair, or pulling basil from between my|my teeth, or anything that begins as fixing.

♦

I read about a woman with dysmorphia whose glance in a mirror begets hours of fixing and fixing and fixing her hair. She keeps her shiny metallic toaster in a cupboard. She keeps her workplace free of reflective surfaces. She lives afraid of mirrors, of what switch they flip in her.

♦

What good are surfaces? Beyond touching, we want to push. We want to tear. Light, as particle and wave, spans both surface and depth. I|I peel back the periphery.

Mirrors do not add new light. They recycle it, the way they recycle my|my face.

I|I amplify my|my sadness gazing at my|my own sad face. Mirror neurons working from the outside in.

♦

It is an inescapable horror, being seen. What begins as want ends at want again. No—ends never—

♦

To make mirrors, silvering lays out the tain, the shine. A rough layer is smoothed with gristmills and grit. Enough etchings make a polish.

Enough seeing and the subject's eyes blur, vision softens. A shine mars sight.

Catoptromancy is the art of divination by polished or reflective surfaces. Sometimes it is understood to refer to divination by mirrors only, as distinguished from divination by other shiny surfaces, such as a polished fingernail.

♦

Mirrors offer more seeing. A deepening of sight. My|My vision opens out, opens into the surfaces of things.

My|My open visions out, unsurfaces things.

Staring, I|I scry to believe in the world in layers.

A design trick: if the subject cannot afford the space they want, the subject can erect a wall of mirrors to give this impression. To open up a room, they say. They mean, to open out a room. Illusion and illumine, sister words.

To determine the best placement for a mirror, centuries ago the interior decorators of the le Pelletier de Saint-Fargeau residence in Paris stood against the wall and looked out the window, painting an exact replica of the landscape on the wall behind them. Mirrors a more perfect portrait.   The outside in.

◆

Every night my|my great-grandmother slathered her face in Vaseline. I|I imagine pillowcases stained clear. White stained to translucency.

Was this to protect her skin from ageing or to protect her skin from her own hands? What stains have I|I inherited?

◆

There are many coping mechanisms, all of which involve covering. Cover my|my hands with cotton gloves. Cover my|my mirror with a scarf. Cover my|my face with concealer. A cover-up: a crime.

Cover: to stain to opacity.

A practice: Stand before the mirror for one minute every day. Morning, evening, afternoon. Do nothing but look. Give attention to the direction of light, the twitching of the hands, the desire to see past two dimensions, the desire to see nothing at all.

See how astonishment curls up around the throat like a mink stole, soft and spined.

There is a museum with a long, winding exhibit of painted mirrors. All the mirrors hang at approximately our height. In each frame there are painted people standing, looking away, looking at the subject, looking down, looking at one another. In the middle of each frame is a patch of mirror left unpainted. Whenever we stand in the middle of each mirror, we are looking at ourselves. We meet our own gaze.

◆

In the museum of mirrors, we meet with the most unfamiliar gaze. The unwound weight of this light from our own two eyes. Framed by vision, structure is sight.

◆

The mirror-paintings reflect only the outer self, but knowing this doesn't keep me from wondering, wandering—sister words. Eyes wander, mind wonders. Eyes widen and gloss with wonder, with water open.

We practice hiding our sadness. We practice hiding our disgust. We practice. And practice in the mirror until the mirror's truth separates from all we know.

At the end of the museum exhibit is a holy water font. One of the docents is a part-time priest, and he blesses the font every morning.

◆

After all those mirrors, the subject cannot help but lean over the font's edge. The subject cannot help but search for our countenance in this new scene, our countenance made holy. Both inner and outer self reformed by water.

A practice: To determine where one experiences oneself, a simple test related to mirror images may be used. When the subject's eyes are closed, try writing the number 3 on their forehead. Ask them, *What do you see in your mind? Is it a 3, or an Ɛ?*

If they see it as an Ɛ, the implication is that it is being seen from a psychological self inside their head. If it is seen as a 3, their psychological self is before their face.

There is some evidence that more men than women see themselves from the outside—from in front of their face—as though they have mirrors watching their own expressions, how they appear to you.

Now that you know the trick to discerning where one experiences the self, you of course can't know yourself. You've seen the trick revealed. Reveal, from the Latin *revēlāre*, to remove the covering from, unveil, to raise the lid of, open. To let light

My husband was sitting on the couch and I asked him to close his eyes. I|I stepped between his legs and lifted his hair to draw a 3 on his forehead with my|my index finger, slowing through the loops. I|I asked him what he saw there. He opened his eyes and said *It depends.* I|I said *No, I mean what did you see there initially. What was your first impulse.*

He said *I'm telling you my first impulse was It depends.*

My|My dog watches himself in the window that turns, at night, into a mirror from the inside. Fact is, windows are mirrors always. All glass reflects some light. Light reflected and untraveling dark. Light and its

♦

motionless lack. In the basement, I|I catch movement out of the corner of my|my eye and start, startle. Underneath a stack of damp, empty boxes, a mirror, lurking. I|I say *lurking* like it waits in shadow for light. Like something that can turn—be turned.

♦

Lurking, from the German *lurken*, to shuffle along, from the Swedish *lurka*, to be slow in one's work, from the Norwegian *lurka*, to sneak away, in the hope of not being seen.

Haunting, of uncertain origin.

Mirror, Mirror on the wall.
Who's the fairest of them all?

Fairest also meaning lightest, brightest, purest. As if light reaches us uncontaminated, emanates undiluted from its nativity.

◆

In Hans Christian Andersen's "Snow Queen," a hobgoblin forges a looking glass hell-bent on warping the truth. His magic mirror shrinks the size of all that is beauty and good, grows the size of all that is bad and worthless. Concave and convex, flexing.

The hobgoblin's mirror transforms a single freckle into a spread

                                                        over

the subject's face entire. Giddy imagining how angels might look in his cursed mirror, the hobgoblin flies his creation up toward heaven. The glass grows slippery with increasing distance from earth. The glass falls. It tumbles, shatters, scatters its sand-grain fragments like freckles over the earth's unblemished face.

These mirror fragments, convinced of their seeing, work their way into subjects' eyes, lodge themselves in subjects' hearts. The fragments wholly transform the subjects' seeing. They harden the cold of the subjects' hearts.

The lungs around their hearts grow dark. Grow heavy. The fragments feed out on light. On looking.

Mirrors recall to us the sole and nightmarish powers we have to hold all of who we are within one frame, lest our minds fly out of our hands and float wide, or crack from side to side. Mind, from the Sanskrit *manas*, the perceptive mind, the perceiver, the sense. The Yoga Sutras teach the separation of *manas* from other qualities of thought and feeling. Healing and wholeness as fragmentation, categories within the self. I|I make space within my|self to better see. The page, the frame is distance.

But my|my thoughts manifest as surface disturbance, as inescapable vision. For Lord Tennyson's Lady of Shalott, so much depends on looking, or not. "Draw near and fear not—" the mirror says. "This is I."

♦

So many tales extend the mirror's seeing beyond reflecting back all that's there, as if even this science will not suffice. Snow White's stepmother might as well have demanded, *Show me the fairest one*, knowing already—having studied her face—that it could not be her.

Shakespeare's King Richard II demands a mirror in Act IV, cries: "A brittle glory shineth in this face: / As brittle as the glory is the face."

He "dashes the glass against the ground," declares it shattered, declares his brittle face destroyed.

♦

The magic of the fairy-tale mirror is its lucidness. It perceives the truth more clearly than the truth can be seen. Its seeing is a truer, clearer seeing.

Mirrors' silence, too, is their honest telling.

Seeing cannot be isolated from thinking. There are several meanings for the verb *see*: *I* see *you driving away; I* see *why you're leaving.* Eye can only receive light. Can only unmake.

◆

Letters are their opposites in a mirror. Each letter's opposite is its sonic opposite, too. The sonic opposite of every letter is pure silence. The sonic opposite of every letter is every letter sounding the same. The mirror means every opposite.

The mouth opens and opens and closes and closes and.

A practice: Use a compact mirror to confirm whether an unconscious person is still breathing. Hold the mirror up to the unconscious person's nose or mouth. Watch the surface of the mirror. If it does not fog,

The Palace of Versailles's Hall of Mirrors contains 357 mirrors bedecking 17 arches. Each arch contains 21 mirrors arranged like windowpanes so as to reflect the palace gardens, to bring the outer world in as light. In 1684, such mirrors were a great luxury.

Luxury, from the Latin *luxus*, abundance, sumptuous enjoyment, from *lux*, light.

◆

In the Hall of Mirrors, restorers chose to leave two etched names in the glass.

Vandalize, from the Latin *vandalus*, to destroy, deface, harm—but originally for wander. I deface by looking away.

◆

Deface, from face, which comes from the Latin *facere*, to make. Also the root of fashion. Also the root of fact.

The face: something I|I make myself. Deface: to unmake.

Part of the reason Romans wanted clear glass in the first place was to see their wine better. Like holding up one hand between eye and light. To see my color more clearly.

◆

In one of Aesop's fables, a dog carrying a bone in his mouth sees his reflection in a pond's quiet water. Thinking his reflection is another dog with a larger bone, the real dog lunges at his reflection while the reflection-dog lunges toward air. Falling in, the real dog disrupts the illusion into punishment.

A doubling that generates loss. How many erroneous hours I|I've spent at surface. How many hours spent wanting and wanting and.

◆

In the mirror, I|I reach. We animal.

Tiresias's prophesy: A long life for beautiful children if we never know ourselves.

Childseeing: we are all beautiful, given in whose image we were made. Children of God. But knowing, and tasting to know from the tree at the heart of Eden, kneeling to kiss the pool of water. Our beauty belies our wanting to consume it.

◆

A curse: the subject is stuck staring. The subject is punished for being-holding beholding themselves. The subject pines for the beauty of their own reflection, for subject|object.

In looking, we know. We begin to burn.

I|I weaponize the mirror. Ancient Greeks theorized that light came from the eyes—something I|I slip into believing when my|my gaze meets with my|my gaze. Sight like beams spills wide and water—but in mirror, foreshortened. The wide cast of my|my gaze shrunk shallow, shrunk point. And no less overwhelm. In fact, like a whittled beam, I|I pierce my|self.

♦

The monstrous Medusa, the Gorgon with snakes for hair, turned all who gazed into her fearsome eyes to stone. In Apollodorus's account, Athena gifted Perseus with a mirrored shield for his pursuit of Medusa. By gazing upon her face at an angle through the shield, Perseus was able to behead her. He was not turned to stone.

One morning after I|I'd picked my|my skin raw, my|my husband stood beside me|me in the bathroom mirror while I|I attempted to cover it up. If the mirror were an instrument of truth, looking at him in the mirror would have felt like a conduit. Instead, it

was the misalignment of air.

Bernardino Ramazzini visited the mirror makers on Murano in Venice in the late 1600s, where craftsmen poured luminous mixtures of tin and mercury atop glass: "Those who make the mirrors become palsied and asthmatic from handling mercury. . . . you may see these workmen . . . scowling at the reflection of their own suffering in their mirrors and cursing the trade they have chosen."

♦

Seeing the reflection of the subject's own suffering magnifies it. Blink in a mirror and it happens twice.

Socrates would hold up mirrors to drunks passing by on the street.

♦

I|I read of a woman afflicted with smallpox who waited months before confronting her alien, pockmarked reflection.

Maybe a mirror's honesty depends.

The first successful photographs were etched by light on mirrors. Louis-Jacque-Mandé Daguerre, creator of the daguerreotype, discovered that one could use silver plates treated with mercury vapor to develop an image. Silver memory mirrors.

◆

When photography was invented and began to appear in news reporting in the 1800s, there was great hope in its reality. People couldn't lie with photography. In his 1840 article "The Daguerreotype," Edgar Allan Poe claimed the photograph would "afford an absolute perspective of objects."

"Perhaps," he said, "if we imagine the distinctness with which an object is reflected in a positively perfect mirror, we come as near the reality as by any other means."

◆

We tell lies to see the mirror reflect them. We trick honesty into illusion. We appear, disappear.

Haunting.

◆

By the early 1860s, photographer William Mumler was creating spirit photographs. He'd take a person's portrait and, after some time in the darkroom, he'd return with a print of the subject and a faint ghost hovering over them. Uncertain origin.

The mirror is haunted by what is not found within its frame.

Artist Frida Kahlo fastened a mirror to the ceiling of her canopy bed while she convalesced, her whole body slowly healing from a gruesome accident. Fastened between bed and mirror, she painted self-portraits.

In 1938, Kahlo gave a mirror she made and a self-portrait to a dear friend, Mary Sklar. The two pieces have matching frames and are to be hung side-by-side as one work. The portrait is a gift of her presence; the mirror so she and Mary could be together always.

♦

Physicist Carlo Rovelli has said that time only makes sense relatively, like how *up* and *down* only make sense relative to being on earth's surface. Rovelli says people are not things, but happenings.

Light isn't matter, but process. A we becoming.

Space telescopes orbit the earth with their hexagonal, interlocking mirrors. The glass must be light. The glass must reflect light.

Light and light: twin words. The adjective meaning of little weight, coming from the Old High German *lungar*, also the root for lung, so called because of the organ's lightness. All an echo of air.

◆

There is a slow and complicated process for magnifying the past without shimmering it. Shimmering is a real risk—telescope mirrors hold onto sunshine's heat, shimmering light in air like the hot exhale above a long summer road. *Mirage* from *mirror*. To combat such distortions of vision, engineers honeycomb the glass beneath the mirror's reflective surface. This glass before the application of surface is called a mirror blank. The honeycomb structure of the mirror blank breathes in, holds the temperature of ambient air, keeping vision clear as maiden skin.

◆

To look farther out is also to look farther back. Light is also its ability to travel.

Astrophysicists' verbs for the movement of light within a telescope: *collect, focus, scatter.*

Light is always see   -king space.
                                                            Becoming.

Honeycomb structure, honeylike melt. To form the big, paraboloid mirrors of a telescope, scientists slowly coax the borosilicate glass to a temperature of 2,156 degrees Fahrenheit, to reach the viscosity of cold honey.

◆

Honeybees' compound eyes are composed of hexagons, the same structure as their honeycomb homes.

This my|my model for creation. A reflection, a duplication. What all I|I deface. Every haunting thing.

A practice: Tell your subject to look in your eyes. Look equally in your subject's eyes. Look therein for your own reflected face.

There is an old theory as to why we fall in love that goes something like this: We see our own reflection in another's eyes.

With their face up to your face, you can see keep hold

In many cases, people with severe dissociative disorders experience discomfort and disorientation when they look at themselves in the mirror. They are unlikely to see a predictable reflection due to the mutability of self-image in multiple personality disorder.

What the subject sees in the mirror is susceptible to consciousness. What we see is consciousness made visible.

♦

The subject's face is opposite in a mirror. It is a widely held belief that more symmetrical faces are more beautiful. Symmetrical faces are not altered by the mirror.

I taught myself to look pretty with a mirror. I|I taught my|self sexy with a mirror. I|I learned by error and error and error

The mirror taught me to look very very closely.

♦

My reflection haunts, always eager to mute my|my gaze.
In the split I, we hear simulacra.   The Eye in Iconography, staring.

The changing nature of the face and the body means the mystery evolves. Like a shadow, the subject is always on her heels.

Unseen: this work of containing.

♦

It's a crisis to constantly manage one's face. The subject|object meets our gaze. The subject is briefly lucid. The object shines.

Before the trifold mirror outside the fitting rooms of a department store, a toddler delights in her image. She dances and waves her arms, giggles and spins.

Children beg their parents for something *again, again*—but before the mirror, she is her

♦

own engine of again. Or the mirror is. They grow indistinguishable.

I|I try to see my|self as a child, have patience with her when she's tired and sorry. In the mirror, the subject eyes the object. This child-seeing means admitting to fracture, admitting the failures of sight, admitting

♦

Memory is a mirror with ambition. Neither has any mercy. I|I close my|my eyes, afraid to resemble.

I|I want to wake from this lucid dream. Lucid from the Latin *lucere*, to shine, an insistence of light.

In standing before the mirror, I|I have my|my moments   of lucidity. Clearly something's gone   wrong. Brief glimpses. A picture develops, emerges from the dark. Little scar flecks, pale little hauntings.

◆

Let me|me be clear: I|I am aware how all this looks. Watch me|me maneuver the nightmare I|I've become.

It's not your seeing, but my|my saying. Language always looking to be held. My|My two ruinous hands.

At night when I|I stare in the bathroom mirror, I|I sometimes turn on the faucet to sound like more than looking. How many baths anyone could have taken in those years of water. How clean all could be.

◆

A mirror surrounds me|me with self. Leaving the room is not an escape. Memory is I|I take my|my image with me|me everywhere I|I

◆

"Cut my shadow from me.
Free me from the torment
of seeing myself without fruit.

"Why was I born among mirrors?"
—FEDERICO GARCÍA LORCA, "Song of the Barren Orange Tree"

If I|I'd been born in a time before glass. Would I|I still be this. Would I|I still find fracture. I|I want to tell her she is hurting me.

Eye or I. But we already see.

◆

Light emanates from destruction. Someone burning. The predicament: every visible object that is not a direct light source is a mirror. Am I|I making my|self clear? All of us little moons, little round faces, reflecting to be seen.

Magnifying mirrors are a cosmetic accessory said to be necessary to elegance and bathroom comfort. Magnifying mirrors seek to close the gap between the subject's pores and the subject's gaze. The farther I|I stand from the mirror, the larger our image. I|I cannot escape the cratered surface of the face.

◆

Mirrors as necessary to comfort—comfort, from the Latin *confortare*, to strengthen. Of the many methods for strengthening, some involve great discomfort.

Glass is stronger in its molten state than it is at room temperature. How uncomfortable, the potential for shatter.

◆

In 1902, American sociologist Charles Cooley theorized what he called "the looking glass self," that we do not know ourselves as a result of others' perceptions, but how we perceive others perceiving us. We look out at looking. We project a reflection.

Everywhere, our subjects' eyes shine us back in.

My|My desire, reflected, becomes shame. The mirror is my|my tool
of disloyalty. I|I refuse to be

here   there
                                                                                                  here
                                                                                                   her

♦

The presence of a mirror elicits shame. Shame is a self-separation.
In giving this face back to me|me, the mirror takes my|my loneliness.
I|I am beside my

                                          self, this mirror between.

♦

"A true citizen of planet earth closes their eyes
and says what they are before the mirror."
—JOSHUA JENNIFER ESPINOZA, "Things Haunt"

I|I don't know that I|I'm a true anything, regardless of how the mirror
hears me|me. I|I exhale to speak. My|My exhale fogs the mirror,
blurs this face, haunts my|my want in looking.

A practice: All day eat only foods and drinks with reflective surfaces.
Suggestions: Coffee. Hot glazed donuts. Waxed apples. Melting
cheese. Glossy broth. Lozenges. Ganache. Before bed, make of
them a list. Circle all the listed vowels. Distill the most common
vowel and write it big on its own piece of paper. Inside your mouth,
find the shape your tongue makes to pronounce this vowel. Fall as-
leep holding this silent shape inside

The first mirror required total stillness of air, a gentle approach. Light touch to pooled liquid surface. Where we got the idea that water was blue.

The creation story is a story of this first mirror. After light, God made the firmament, and divided the waters which were under the firmament from the waters which were above the firmament. Both true water. And it was so that we were to live in this space between two waters, between two surfaces blistering light.

◆

The possibilities of light. The world f   ills to the brim with dawn.

◆

The site of all seen—the divinity, the repulsiveness—in us, an image. How radiant the subject grows, seeing ourselves, simulacra of all. Divine liminality.

The mirror is the central object of a Shinto shrine. An instrument for contemplation.

The individual gaze is not physical. Instead, it penetrates the physical into the innermost, mystical self.

Pierce myself to see into the soul.

♦

The mirror is a sacred object. The mirror gestures toward eternity the way two hands pressing evoke prayer. Two must join—the divine and the image, the left and the right, the subject|object. Between: parallax.

The early church banned the use of the mirror because its reflection was known to trigger hypnosis, a trance state. The subject their own object of affection. Mirror, a frame around my attention.

◆

Sight, the origin

of sin. Light, the origin

of world. What a bind, unsought, the seeing are

in.

◆

Christian pilgrims in the seventeenth century bring with them small hand-mirrors and hold them up to sacred relics, to the light, to the angle of light to their eyes. They briefly capture the sacred within the frame. The mirror is thought to hold all it's seen. Miracle.

In the 1200s, Jean de Meun wrote in *Roman de la Rose* about God's mirror as the primary tool of predestination. "This mirror is the same one from which we took our beginning," he says. "In this beautiful polished mirror, which He keeps and has always kept with Him ... He sees all that will happen and will keep it always present."

Everything within the frame. Everything the mirror keeps present.

◆

Is God not Narcissus, having made from His own image and then stuck staring?

What object am I to think my|self subject? Subjected to this staring again and again and.

◆

Prophecy is the ability to see with clarity, then speak.

God saw the light, that it was good. God has seen in every direction, one of which is away.

After the funeral of an immediate relative, as per Jewish custom, all mirrors are to be covered in the house of mourning for seven days. This, according to Kabbalists, keeps the mourners from facing any demons in the mirror.

◆

In one version of the story of Narcissus, the boy is mourning the death of his twin sister when he comes upon his reflection. What he sees in the water is not merely his face, but hers—their inheritance. Her come alive again in their mother's nose, their father's lips, their grandfather's eyes, their grandmother's cheeks.

All are born but a poor reflection.

◆

The Godhead, a light source, a face to shine upon you. Across the great divine distance, an ancestry of faces. So much to mourn. So many distant, heavy hours.

◆

Mourning leaves us vulnerable. In the mirror, I|I am always mourning a face I|I no longer have. Every morning I|I cover my|my mirror. Every morning a mourning.

A practice: In a large room cleared of its furniture, hang a mirror at the height of your face on the wall. Standing at the mirror, affix two pieces of paper with tape just above and below your head on the mirror's surface. Now back up. Walk backward again, holding the gaze of your reflection-face. Your face will continue to occupy the same space as it did when you were standing close. The mirror will fail to reflect any more of yourbody than your face.

Obsession is the law of reflection, or its result. This insistence.

I want sobriety from my body, to be clean of my|my body's compulsions—my|my hands, my|my fingernails, my|my skin never quite smooth. I|I am my|my own weapon: Medusa whose snake tresses turn their fangs to the flesh of her own soft cheeks. Medusa whose jawline is overlapping puncture wounds. The choice between severing each serpent— whose bones are mine, whose blood is my|my own—or looking past the pain of their betrayal, the pain of this visibility.

I|I hone my|my own hurt.

◆

Medusa wanting to kill herself. Medusa needing to gaze into her own eyes. The most obvious way of doing so, in a mirror, not working. Illusion is safe, the gods nearly saying.

Instead, Medusa begging Perseus to use the mirror to do it. Perseus watching as he slayed her in the mirror's reflection. Perseus the hero. Medusa monstrous.

Blood is easily cleaned from a mirror.

Now and now, in front of the mirror, little experiments with my|my mortality: I|I control my|my pain 👁 make.

◆

Every day I|I approach disfigurement like a diligent wish.

There is no need to tell me I|I'm wrong, doctor. We can both see.

They promised me|me skin like silk and smooth. Skin like milk and fair. Skin so creamy and opalescent I|I must have poured it on. I|I have purchased such promises for a pretty penny. I|I have scrubbed and patted and blotted and blended. Tweezed and bleached and blushed and brushed. If this were a practice, I|I would be good by now. But culture buffs shame to ritual. I|I genuflect at the bathroom sink, at mirror's edge. This is my|my days' ending, beginning. I|I cannot parse out what part of cleansing becomes sin, cannot excise any purity from

Scabs cling to my|my skin like shells to shore. I|I line them up on the edge of the sink. I|I make patterns where there was chaos before: a whole ocean, a whole landscape unbreathing beneath it.

There is a power in destroying my|self, but it is less than the power of not having to.

Looking into a mirror is an out-of-body experience, an autoscopy. The brain cannot make sense of the face from without, attempts to locate consciousness with the parallax of the inner ears and the mirror's surface.

A common perspective in autoscopy is the bird's-eye view—seeing oneself from above. To leave the physical body and all its maladies only to be stuck gazing at it. No refuge from the self, always in its frame.

Disappoint. From the French *disappointer*, to strip someone of their clothes, or to deprive them of a position. When I|I disappoint you, I|I am removing you from the position of holding some certain belief: that I|I am well, that I|I look after my|self, that my|my beauty is genuine, that I|I do not suffer. That this fire is not mine.

To deprive of a position could mean I|I destroy it. It could mean I|I add it to the blaze.

◆

I|I deprive you. Deprive, sister of private, from the Latin *privus*, single or individual. Deprive: to take away, withdraw, to cut off or remove someone from something. Its history is violence—that when I|I deprive you, I|I am withdrawing your individuality. Or I|I am taking you from the world, that your individuality only exists within the frame of public life. In private, I|I am deprived. Shame thrives in a deprived state.

◆

When I|I first told her about my|my dermatillomania, my|my mother cried. She wanted to know what she could have done to cause it, what she could have done better to stop it. Either logic worked.

I|I didn't want to share my|my disappointment. I|I wanted to deprive my|self alone. I|I was so used to my|my disappointment. Hers deprived me|me of its loneliness.

In a yoga class, I|I heard a woman confess that she thought her pregnancies would cure her of anorexia. They didn't, granting instead a deeper nuance to her dysmorphia, knowing her body was capable of growing then birthing then nursing and still seeing wrong, seeing fat.

I|I confess that I|I, too, have held this hope—that being pregnant might purify me|me of my|my desire to cause my|self harm, that seeing my|self as a vessel for another would keep me|me from hurting my|my child, thus from hurting my|self.

Hope is familiar. I|I have held so many, all of which I|I've ruined.

◆

The yoga studio in which the workshop took place had a wall of mirrors. I|I had been going there for a year before I|I even knew they were mirrors because they were assiduously concealed by crimson fabric featuring vertical lines of large white flowers. The studio owner told me|me later that she only removed the fabric in certain workshops where seeing one's anatomical alignment was key; otherwise, she kept the whole wall of them hidden. I|I wondered if the pregnant anorexic woman knew of this kindness, the covered mirrors.

Sometimes, in class, if I|I paid close enough attention, I|I could just barely make out the outline of my|my reflection, like the ghost of an afterimage, a shadow behind the curtain.

◆

In mirrored rooms, everything everything happens and nothing nothing is recorded.

A 1968 experiment determined that most people can hallucinate when they stare at their own reflections in a mirror. To fall into a trance state. Trance, from the Old French *transir*, to depart, from the Latin *transire*, to go across.

A trance is the psyche split. Subject|Object. The other in the self. Particle and wave.

A physics joke found on T-shirts and sandwich boards outside quirky coffee shops goes like this: "You matter. Unless you multiply yourself by the speed of light squared. Then you energy." $e=mc^2$, meaning all mass has the potential for energy, seen as light. As color.

In mirrors, light is all we are. Vision our end.

A practice: To engage a baby's developing vision, place a flexible plastic nontoxic mirror in front of the baby during tummy time. The baby can babble, giggle, play peekaboo with their reflection until about two years of age, when self-conception begins to psychologically emerge. The self as themselves. The body as thembodies.

Researchers have tested human babies' and other animals' ability to recognize their mirror image as themselves by applying a spot of rosy blush to their faces. A defect. Humans, chimps, bonobos, orangutans, and elephants all reach for the defect on their faces. They all subject themselves. To touch the defect here is a sign of intelligence, of self-concept. The mirror stage. Dolphins, without hands to touch the defect, instead give close attention to the mark on their bodies with the aid of a mirror. Without hands, the mark remains. Stains.

◆

Chimps raised in total social isolation from other chimps failed the mirror test.

Without other,

object.

Hours of isolation from others pull me to my face, help ensure the isolation continues. There is always a defect.

I look to the moon, but her eyes are only scars.

The moon remains the same, with or without the light that is not hers. What I|I'm saying is that it's not my|my language in my|my mouth. Words are reflections. Their color's in the saying, the scrying.

What I|I fear: irrevocable damage. To my|my relationships, my|my planet, my|my face. How faces over time become us—even to ourselves—

The other night my|my husband, walking past, gestured to the scarf draped over the bathroom mirror. *This is good. It's working,* he said.

I|I called after him, *But every time I put it up, I have to admit that I can't do this myself.*

Well, he called back, *humans are fallible; systems are not.*

All my|my many systems. Systems of practices. A belief becoming.

A practice: one way to intentionally conduct my|body toward hope.

◆

On a page, there is room for forgiveness. There is space. To say, then see the saying. The blessing of literacy is its lag.

Childseeing

                                    holding all I|I've seen
                                         means admitting
                                            to time

across which light waves.
across which I|I forgive.

A process becomes ritual. The subject crosses over.

A practice: The brain continues seeing even after the stimulus has been removed. Stare at these words for ten unmoving seconds, then quickly shift the gaze to the blank white page, where ghost type will appear.

Even closing the eyes is no immediate escape from vision. The afterimage ghosts your eyelids, haunts like a ghost come in through the door you would not have left open had you known there was a ghost out there. How could you have.

Totally self-contained is what we call beautiful. A frame around a mirror.

The frame severs what's inside from the whole. My body the boundary of my becoming, though fractal, unsurfaced.

♦

Leonardo da Vinci once said, "No body is in itself defined in the mirror; but the eye on seeing it in this mirror puts boundaries to it."

Some insist God didn't design us to see ourselves.

Vision is always limited. Language has its dimension. The page. The frame. The body.

A mirror reflects even its own surface. The gap is an illusion of distance doubled. Not just space between the surface and its backing, but all that seen twice, light coursing through it again.

Everything in this universe caught up in a lag. Expanded time. Swell of space across which light waves.

The moon knows her luminous face; she watches it glide over oceans. See, sea—sister words. The moon's yearning tugs at every ocean's weight, fractures it to waves.

It is not loneliness that calls out her longing—it is seeing her light, and having no way to hold

Time has a way of making the subject feel like they get to etch themselves into what's left of before. There is a way to be present without being the absence of what's already here. It is the way of light.

Call into being all everywheres.　　　　　No where without light.

A practice sanctioned by Jesus: Put your fingers into your wounds. Worry yourself open. Make yourbody transparent in spots. Like there is a truest layer, a deepest surface.

Oh little wounds, little faith. Belief: Scry again and

Some faith traditions believe that pain causes evil to leave the body. Redemptive, purifying pain. The glowing coal sears Isaiah's lips clean. The crucifixion is God self-flagellating. Godflesh mortified.

Purifying, cousin of purgatory, place from which no one originates. What true purity has any origin?

The fire catches the bush. Who's to say it does not feel the burning?

The pain inflicted on Jesus was payment. Self-flagellation: the practice of cleansing the soul of the body's many guilts. A performance of remorse.

In this mode, is the act of self-inflicting pain ever a sin, or just its opposite?

Opposite, flipped.   A kind of reflection.

After standing before the mirror for a lost hour, I'm mortified. For-getting my makeup on a weekend trip, mortified. A small child asks me in front of his mother what's wrong with my face. I feel her glowing mortification for my sake.

Mortified, from the Latin *mortificare*, to kill or subdue, from *mort-*, death.

Mortification of the flesh is an act by which a believer puts to death their sinful nature, as a part of the process of sanctification. Holy-making.

I am my own cilice. I wear me down. Using the body to escape the body, briefly. A baptism of beestings. A baptism of beatings. To choose one's wounds, like Jesus. Who wouldn't stumble under the weight?

Death, a cleansing. Washing the body from the soul.

I take a bite of the scroll, but it is bitter and dry.

I break out
of me—

When does compulsion cross over into tradition?

A practice II's the subject.

Amiisafe Amiisafe Amiisafe   ?

II searches. MyMy body in wait.

II mortify mymyself mymybody. II threat and II victim. It is not safe to leave mæne with mæne.

A practice: On a summer evening, I find a meadow. I walk to its middle, roughly. Turn slowly in a circle, breathing, watching the perimeter. Then change directions—circling, breathing, watching. I do this as many times as I need to convince my self that I am safe here in this meadow.

Once landed in safety, I close my eyes. Remember every way I have thought to end my self. At each remembrance, I come back to the safety of my meadowbody. Open my eyes. Begin the ends.

1. T my arms out, lift my heels to lean forward. Fall from some deadly height. Collapse to my side. Inhale on the ground. Exhale on the ground.

Rise. Repeat the circle of safety in this meadowbody.

2. My left hand the gun, my finger set against the roof of my mouth. I release the safety. Say click. Squeeze the trigger. Shout the shot. Collapse. Inhale on the ground. Exhale on the ground.

Rise. Circle of safety. Meadowbody meadowbody.

3. One hand grips the bottle. Another uncaps the childproof lid. I pour them into my palm. Little wounds. Set down the bottle. Swallow two dozen, two at a time. Water after. Sit in the meadow. Lie fetal, eyes closed. Inhale on the ground. Exhale on the ground.

Rise. Affirm safety. Affirm meadowbody.

4. Hands at ten and two on the steering wheel. Foot on the gas, hard. The speedometer reaching 90. 100. Nearing 110. I jerk the wheel. Shout the crash. Tumble in the grass, rolling, rolling, rolling. I slow, then still. Inhale on the ground. Exhale on the ground.

Rise. Circle. Periphery the body. Frame the safe I.

5. Sit down in the tub. Uncap the razor blade. Turn off the water. Grasp the handle firm. One wrist, side to side. Two. Wincing. Flayed wrists to the sky, lie down. Close my eyes. Inhale on the ground. Exhale on the ground.

Rise again with the inhale.

Rise and
body   again:

Breathe.

Circle arms around (mybody). A forest around a meadow. A sky around a season. Circle of (my chest) around the air, of the air around (mybody).

(I) let night. (I) let starlight.

(I) refuse to put anything to death.

(Everything I am)   between these horizons.

The wave unending.   At its edge, light.

Light travels and this is a miracle. The unrelenting push and pull of bright. Light takes up space. Light takes. Light shines through dimensionality and in its directional shine calls into being the across

of time. Seeing is the world

haunting the body. If only it were this clear: Sight so precise (you and I) call it a line.

(I take space) as birthright.

(My lines) like years, like our living unwound, outstretched.

(I hold our wounds) for their lucid layer. Our deepest surface.

The face our home country. We are each so many. Turn us ever so slightly to see our color change then change.

Seeing (bodies me in)to being. Briefly, a filter over every face.

Every us glimmers. We hums glass.

A note on the use of the punctuation throughout. In mathematics, the upright or vertical slash (|) can denote divisibility, as in the figure on the left divides the figure on the right, or the figure on the left is a factor of the one on the right. In logic, the vertical slash is referred to as the Sheffer stroke, where it means *nand*, or *not and*. Either of the figures astride the Sheffer stroke can be true, or neither can be true, but both cannot be simultaneously true.

In addition, in mathematics, parentheses denote a change in the order of operations by indicating what needs to be evaluated first.

Sometimes periods are not used at the ends of sentences where they would normally appear. And some sentences in the interrogative grammatical mood are punctuated with periods rather than question marks. Both practices are intentional.

All etymologies mentioned are sourced from the *Oxford English Dictionary*, Third Edition.

Page 2: "There is no objective mirror" is a quote from page 244 of Sabine Melchior-Bonnet's book *The Mirror: A History*, translated from the French by Katharine H. Jewett (Routledge, 2001).

Page 6: The second section references a woman featured on page 359 of Mark Pendergrast's book *Mirror Mirror* (Basic Books, 2003): "Psychiatrist Katharine Phillips . . . in her 1996 book, *The Broken Mirror* . . . quotes Sarah, a third-year medical student with 'body dysmorphic disorder,' a form of OCD in which she cannot stop trying to 'fix' her hair for hours. 'I try not to ever look in the mirror when I'm at work, because when I do I can get stuck there,' Sarah says. 'The mirror acts like a switch. When I look in, the obsession turns on, and it can get pretty out of control,' so bad that she keeps her shiny toaster hidden in a cupboard at home."

Page 8: "Catoptromancy is the art of divination by polished or reflective surfaces. Sometimes it is understood to refer to divination by mirrors only, as distinguished from divination by other shiny surfaces, such as a polished fingernail" is a quote from Claire Fanger's paper "Virgin Territory: Purity and Divine Knowledge in Late Medieval Catoptromantic Texts" in the journal *Aries*, 5, no. 2, (July 2005): 200–224.

Page 13: This "simple test" and some of its language come from page 10 of Richard Gregory's book *Mirrors in Mind* (Penguin, 1997).

Page 20: The disparate meanings of the verb *see* as well as the phrase that the eye can "only receive light" come from pages 214–215 of Richard Gregory's *Mirrors in Mind* (Penguin, 1997).

Page 22: Information about the Palace of Versailles's Hall of Mirrors and some of the language in the first stanza come from the Château de Versailles's website's "The Hall of Mirrors" webpage (en.chateauversailles .fr/discover/estate/palace/hall-mirrors).

Page 26: The quote from Bernardino Ramazzini's visit to the mirror makers at Murano comes from *De Morbis Artificum Diatriba* (1700, 1713).

Page 28: The sentence "The first successful photographs were etched by light on mirrors" and the phrase "silver memory mirrors" come from page 174 of Richard Gregory's *Mirrors in Mind* (Penguin, 1997).

The sentence "The mirror [is] haunted by what is not found within it[s frame]" is a quote from page 273 of Sabine Melchior-Bonnet's *The Mirror: A History*, translated by Katharine H. Jewett (Routledge, 2001).

Page 30: The information about Frida Kahlo's *Fulang-Chang and I* comes from the Museum of Modern Art (MoMA)'s website (www.moma.org/ explore/inside_out/2009/12/03/a-close-look-frida-kahlo-s-fulang-chang- and-i).

On the March 16, 2017 episode of Krista Tippett's podcast *On Being*, Carlo Rovelli said, "I think that time is an approximate thing, not a fundamental thing, in the world—like up and down: Up and down makes sense here on Earth, but not in space." In the episode, Tippett mentions that Rovelli says in his book *Seven Brief Lessons on Physics* that we are in "a world of happenings, not of things." Rovelli elaborates, "Yes, a thing is something which remains equal to itself. A stone is a thing because I can ask where the stone is tomorrow, while a happening is something that is limited in space and time. A kiss is not a thing, because I cannot ask, where is a kiss, tomorrow; 'Where is this kiss?' tomorrow. I mean, it's just happened now.... And I think that we don't understand the world as made by stones, by things. We understand the world made by kisses, or things like kisses—happenings. In other words, the elementary quantities or ingredients for describing the world are not things which remain through time; they are just limited in space and time. And I think which remain through time are processes that repeat themselves. . . . So to better understand the world, I think, we shouldn't reduce it to things. We should reduce it to happenings; and the happenings are always between different systems, always relations, or always like a kiss, which is something that happens between two persons."

Page 30: A 2014 *National Geographic* video on YouTube called *Go Inside a Telescope Mirror Factory | To a Billionth of a Meter* visits the University of Arizona's Mirror Lab. In interviews, the scientists there describe the process of working with honeycombed mirror blanks and shimmering that can happen to images when mirrors hold onto heat longer than the surrounding air (www.youtube.com/watch?v=MjUcBWYVF9s).

The verbs "collect, focus, scatter" come from the FAQ page on the website for the University of Arizona's Richard F. Caris Mirror Lab (mirrorlab.arizona.edu/content/faq), which says, "The surface of a telescope mirror must be polished to its precise paraboloidal shape within approximately 1/25 of the wavelength of light. For typical blue light, that means a surface accuracy of order 15–20 nanometers (less than 1.0 × inch). Any small scale roughness (the lack of a good polish) will cause the light to be scattered and result in reduced contrast. Inaccuracies on larger scales, such as bending of the entire mirror, can result in an inability to focus the light into sharp images. The value of these large mirrors in telescopes is to collect lots of light from very faint astronomical objects and to focus it into very sharp images."

Page 32: The idea that "Honeybees' compound eyes are composed of hexagons, the same structure as their honeycomb homes" comes from an October 25, 2013 *Smithsonian* article by Joseph Stromberg called "What Does a Bee Look Like When It's Magnified 3000 Times?" In the article, photographer Rose-Lynn Fisher says, "In that first moment, when I saw its eye, I realized that the bees' eyes are composed of hexagons, which echo the structure of the honeycomb. . . . I stood there, just thinking about that, and how there are these geometrical patterns in nature that just keep on repeating themselves" (www.smithsonianmag.com/science-nature/what-does-a-bee-look-like-when-its-magnified-3000-times-555 3827).

Page 34: The passage "In many cases, people with severe dissociative disorders experience discomfort and disorientation when they look at themselves in the mirror. They are unlikely to see a predictable reflection due to the mutability of self-image in multiple personality disorder" comes from page 4 of Richard Gregory's *Mirrors in Mind* (Penguin, 1997).

Page 36: "Memory [is] a mirror with ambition" and "I closed my eyes, afraid to resemble," from Rosmarie Waldrop's poetry collection *The Reproduction of Profiles* (New Directions, 1987), inspire similar phrases here.

Page 38: The Lorca poem "Song of the Barren Orange Tree," as quoted here, was translated by W. S. Merwin.

"Every visible object that is not a direct light source is a mirror" comes from page 69 of Mark Pendergrast's *Mirror Mirror* (Basic Books, 2003). The full quotation is ". . . every visible object that is not a direct light source is a kind of mirror, because light bounces off of it."

Page 40: "The presence of a mirror elicits shame" comes from C. Dylan Bassett's collection *The Invention of Monsters / Plays for the Theatre* (Plays Inverse Press, 2015).

Page 42: "God made the firmament, and divided the waters which were under the firmament from the waters which were above the firmament. . . . And it was so" is from Genesis 1:7, the King James Version (KJV).

Page 43: Information about the mirror being the central object of a Shinto shrine comes from Alan Mcfarlane and Gerry Martin's book *The Glass Bathyscaphe* (Profile Books, 2003).

Page 44: "The early church banned the use of the mirror because its reflection was known to trigger hypnosis, a trance state" was inspired by information from page 189 of Sabine Melchior-Bonnet's book *The Mirror: A History*, translated by Katharine H. Jewett (Routledge, 2001).

Information about Christian pilgrims' handheld mirrors in the seventeenth century comes from the 2014 episode of the PBS series *How We Got to Now* by Paul Olding called "Glass."

Page 44: "And God saw the light, that it was good" is from the beginning of Genesis 1:4 (KJV).

Page 45: The phrases "after the funeral of an immediate relative" and "house of mourning," as well as the information about the Kabbalist tradition of mourning and covering mirrors, come from Chabad.org (www.chabad .org/library/article_cdo/aid/2969340/jewish/Why-Are-the-Mirrors-Covered-in-a-House-of-Mourning.htm).

The phrase "face to shine upon you" comes from Numbers 6:24–26, the English Standard Version: "The Lord bless you and keep you; the Lord make his face to shine upon you and be gracious to you; the Lord lift up his countenance upon you and give you peace."

Page 47: The idea for this practice came from a passage on page 355 of Mark Pendergrast's *Mirror Mirror* (Basic, Books, 2003) on the law of reflection.

Page 54: "In mirrored rooms, everything everything happens and nothing nothing is recorded" is inspired by Jorge Luis Borges's poem "Mirrors": "Everything happens and nothing is recorded / In these rooms of the looking glass." Translated by Mildred Boyer and Harold Morland in *Dreamtigers* (University of Texas Press, 1964).

Page 55: "A 1968 experiment shows how most people can hallucinate when staring at themselves in a mirror" is a quote from page 361 of Mark Pendergrast's *Mirror Mirror* (Basic Books, 2003).

Page 56: Some of the language from "To engage a baby's developing vision" to "baby can babble, giggle, play peekaboo with their reflection" comes from the Amazon.com listing for "Sassy Tummy Time Floor Mirror |

Developmental Baby Toy" (www.amazon.com/Hamco-80030-Sassy-Floor-Mirror/dp/B002J4U8M0).

Page 57: The "mark test" described here was designed by Gordon Gallup. More information about the tests can be found on page 366 of Mark Pendergrast's *Mirror Mirror* (Basic Books, 2003).

Page 62: "Totally self-contained is what we call beautiful" comes from page 71 of C. Dylan Bassett's collection *The Invention of Monsters / Plays for the Theatre* (Plays Inverse Press, 2015).

Leonardo da Vinci's quote comes from *The Notebooks of Leonardo da Vinci: Arranged, Rendered into English and Introduced by Edward MacCurdy*, volume II (Garden City Publishing Co., 1941).

Page 65: This "practice" is "sanctioned by Jesus" because Jesus instructs His doubting disciple, Thomas, to do so in order to believe that Jesus has risen from the dead after His crucifixion. In John 20:25, the New International Version (NIV), Thomas tells his fellow disciples, "Unless I see the nail marks in his hands and put my finger where the nails were, and put my hand into his side, I will not believe." In John 20:27 (NIV), Jesus says to Thomas, "Put your finger here; see my hands. Reach out your hand and put it into my side. Stop doubting and believe."

The phrase "little faith" comes from Jesus's words in Matthew 8:26 (NIV) before He calms a storm: "You of little faith, why are you so afraid?"

Page 67: "Mortification of the flesh is an act by which a believer puts to death their sinful nature, as a part of the process of sanctification" is a paraphrase of a passage of the Wikipedia article on "Mortification of the flesh," which begins, "Mortification of the flesh is an act by which an individual or group seeks to mortify, or put to death, their sinful nature, as a part of the process of sanctification" (en.wikipedia.org/wiki/Mortification_of_the_flesh).

"I take a bite of the scroll, but it is bitter and dry" is an allusion to Ezekiel 2:8–3:3 (NIV): "'But you, son of man, listen to what I say to you. Do not rebel like that rebellious people; open your mouth and eat what I give you.' Then I looked, and I saw a hand stretched out to me. In it was a scroll, which he unrolled before me. On both sides of it were written words of lament and mourning and woe. And he said to me, 'Son of man, eat what is before you, eat this scroll; then go and speak to the people of Israel.' So I opened my mouth, and he gave me the scroll to eat. Then he said to me, 'Son of man, eat this scroll I am giving you and fill your stomach with it.' So I ate it, and it tasted as sweet as honey in my mouth."

RESOURCES

Reader, you are never alone. As with any health issue, seeking treatment quickly for mental health can make all the difference. Please take advantage of any of the below resources:

For help with suicidal crisis, emotional distress, or self-harm, please call the National Suicide Prevention Lifeline at 1-800-273-8255 at any time, or visit their website at suicidepreventionlifeline.org.

For support and resources for body-focused repetitive behaviors (BFRBs) such as trichotillomania, skin picking, nail biting, and more, please visit the TLC Foundation: www.bfrb.org.

For support and resources specifically for skin picking or dermatillomania, please visit the Picking Me Foundation: pickingme.org.

ACKNOWLEDGMENTS

Thank you to Kazim Ali for giving this book a place in the world. My deep, enduring gratitude to everyone at Seneca Review Books: Geoffrey Babbitt, Danny Schonning, the Acquisitions Editorial Board, McKayla Okoniewski, Kylie Rowland, Irini Konstantinou, Tina Smaldone, Laura Glenn, Jeff Clark, Jenny Boully, and Megan Posco, who have all worked tirelessly to make this book a reality. Thank you.

Thank you to all my teachers, but most especially to Dan Beachy-Quick, Matthew Cooperman, Camille Dungy, Stephanie G'Schwind, and Sasha Steensen. Thank you to Diana Khoi Nguyen, Radha Marcum, and all the wonderful folks at Lighthouse Writers Workshop.

Special thanks to Erich Schweikher and everyone at COAST|no-COAST for believing in this project before I dared believe in it myself. Thank you to Nano Taggart and Natalie Young for your support and encouragement.

I am forever grateful to all the generous souls who skillfully guided this manuscript from its earliest stages: Emma Hyche, Kristin Macintyre, Christa Helton Shively, Kelly Weber, Sam Killmeyer, Cole Konopka, David Mucklow, Ryann Peats, Zach Yanowitz, Catie Young, Sarah Wernsing, Margaret Browne, Susannah Lodge-Rigal, Danny Schonning once again, and Kathryn Knight Sonntag.

Thank you to my family. For you, not a blessing, but a prayer of gratitude: Mom, Dad, Margaret, Will, Libby, Ben, and Sam, amen.

And to Matt and Clara: my heart, my home. All my love forever.

ABOUT THE AUTHOR

Katherine Indermaur is the author of two chapbooks, *Facing the Mirror: An Essay* (COAST|noCOAST, 2021) and *Pulse* (Ghost City Press, 2018). She is the winner of the *Black Warrior Review* 2019 Poetry Contest and the 2018 Academy of American Poets Prize, and was named a runner-up in the 92Y's 2020 Discovery Poetry Contest. Her writing has appeared in *Ecotone, Frontier Poetry,* the *Journal, New Delta Review,* the *Normal School, Seneca Review,* and elsewhere. Katherine holds an MFA from Colorado State University and serves as an editor for *Sugar House Review.* She lives with her family in Fort Collins, Colorado.